THE LITTLEST KINDERGARTEN WORKBOOK

This is a book for children who are getting ready to learn how to read and write. The art and logic activities are designed to prepare the child with the skills necessary for reading, writing, spelling and symbolic learning.

BE AN EXAMPLE TO YOUR CHILD.

In order for children to learn how to write they need to see adults writing. Many parents use digital devices and do not write very often with a pen or pencil. Show your child how to make up a story, write it down, and use a pen or pencil.

There are some blank areas so you can draw with your child, or they can be creative. Give your child a black gel pen to finish the logic puzzles in this book. Use gel pens and colored
pencils to color the drawings.

The Thinking Tree, LLC
Copyright 2017 – Do Not Copy

I SPY - FUN-SCHOOLING GAME

CHALLENGE your child to find any item in this picture.

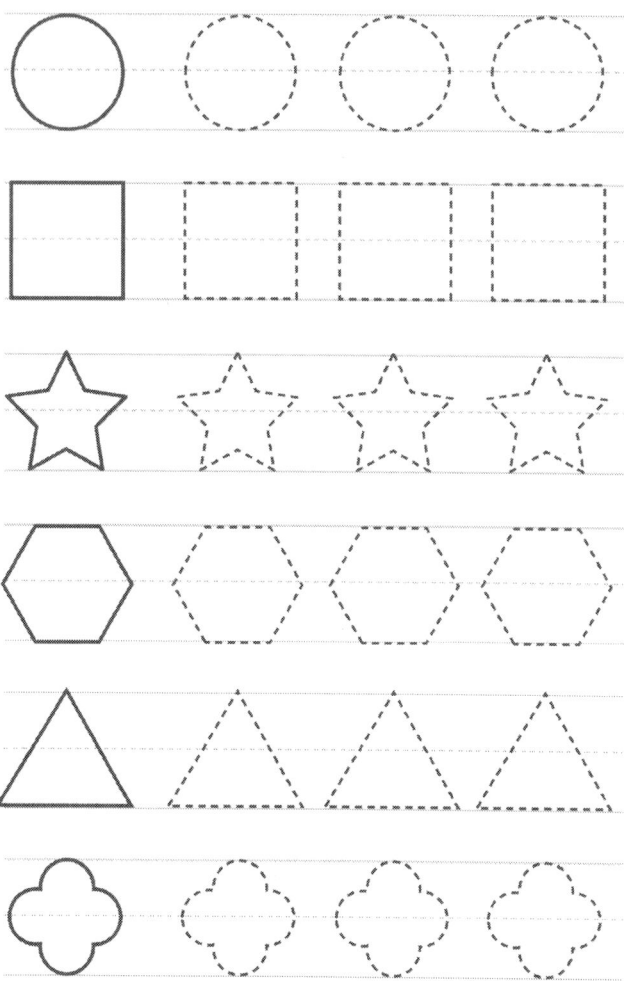

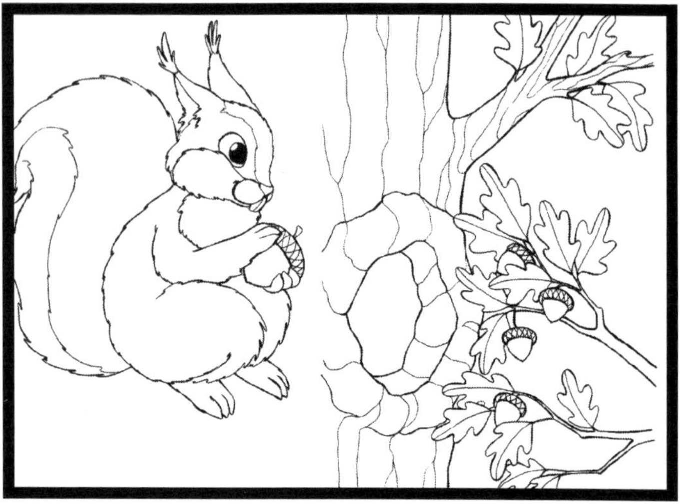

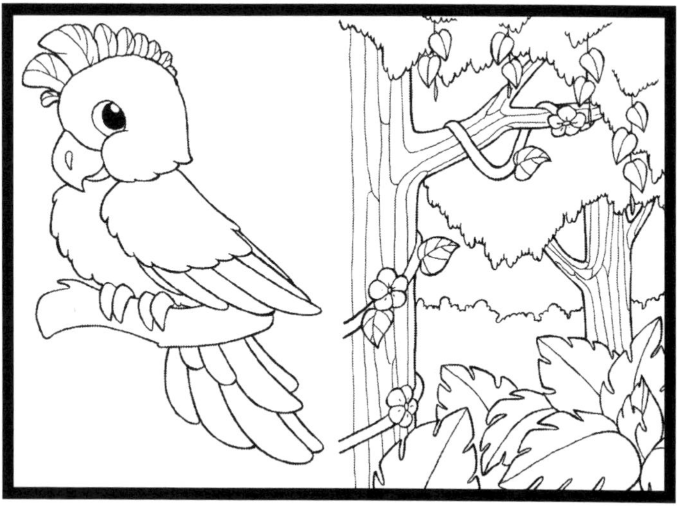

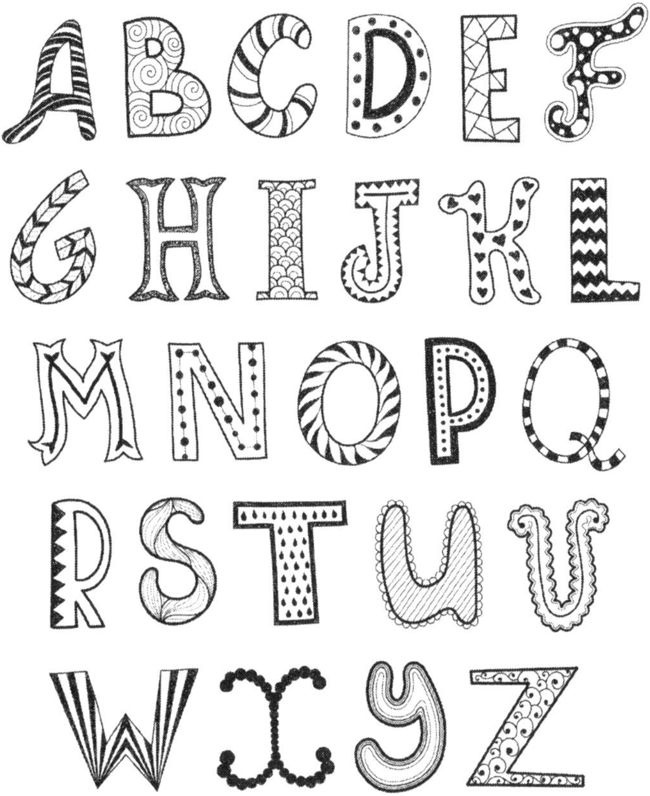
ABCDEF
GHIJKL
MNOPQ
RSTUV
WXYZ

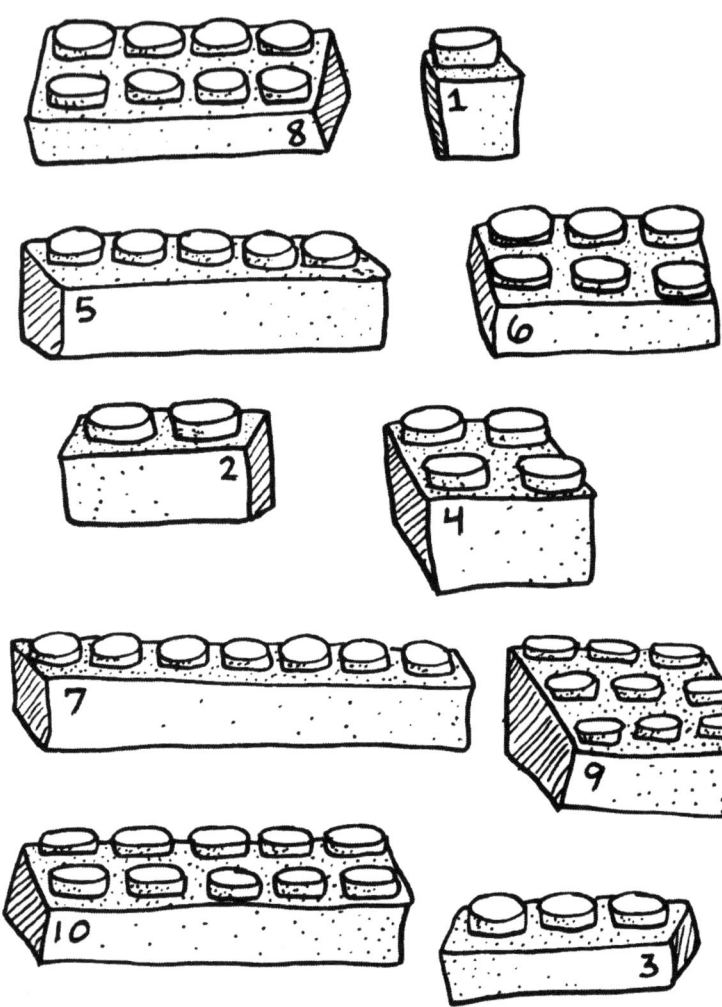

0 0 0 0 0 0 0 0 0
1 1 1 1 1 1 1 1 1
2 2 2 2 2 2 2 2 2
3 3 3 3 3 3 3 3 3
4 4 4 4 4 4 4 4 4
5 5 5 5 5 5 5 5 5
6 6 6 6 6 6 6 6 6
7 7 7 7 7 7 7 7 7
8 8 8 8 8 8 8 8 8
9 9 9 9 9 9 9 9 9

The child can use a black pen to draw the missing parts.

Aa Bb Cc Dd Ee
Ff Gg Hh Ii Jj
Kk Ll Mm Nn
Oo Pp Qq Rr
Ss Tt Uu Vv
Ww Xx Yy Zz

RACCOON

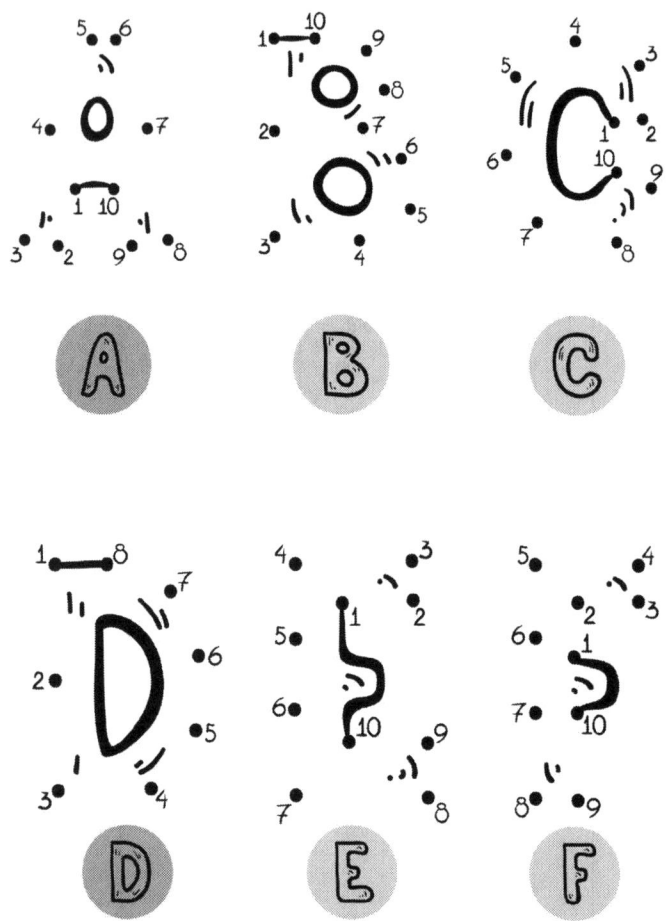

ALL THINGS BRIGHT AND BEAUTIFUL
~CECIL FRANCES ALEXANDER

All things bright and beautiful,
All creatures great and small,
All things wise and wonderful,
The Lord God made them all.

Each little flower that opens,
Each little bird that sings,
He made their glowing colors,
He made their tiny wings.

The purple-headed mountain,
The river running by,
The sunset, and the morning,
That brightens up the sky;

The cold wind in the winter,
The pleasant summer sun,
The ripe fruits in the garden,
He made them every one.

He gave us eyes to see them,
And lips that we might tell,
How great is God Almighty,
Who has made all things well.

HEDGEHOGS

ABCDEF
GHIJKL
MNOPQ
RSTUV
WXYZ

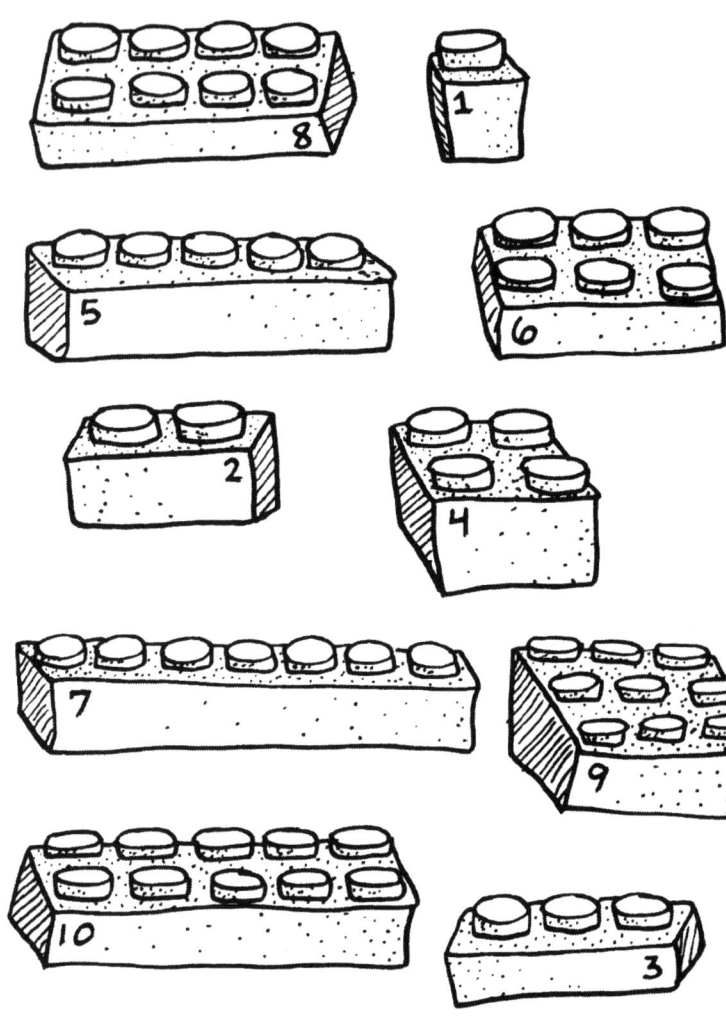

0 0 0 0 0 0 0 0
1 1 1 1 1 1 1 1
2 2 2 2 2 2 2 2
3 3 3 3 3 3 3 3
4 4 4 4 4 4 4 4
5 5 5 5 5 5 5 5
6 6 6 6 6 6 6 6
7 7 7 7 7 7 7 7
8 8 8 8 8 8 8 8
9 9 9 9 9 9 9 9

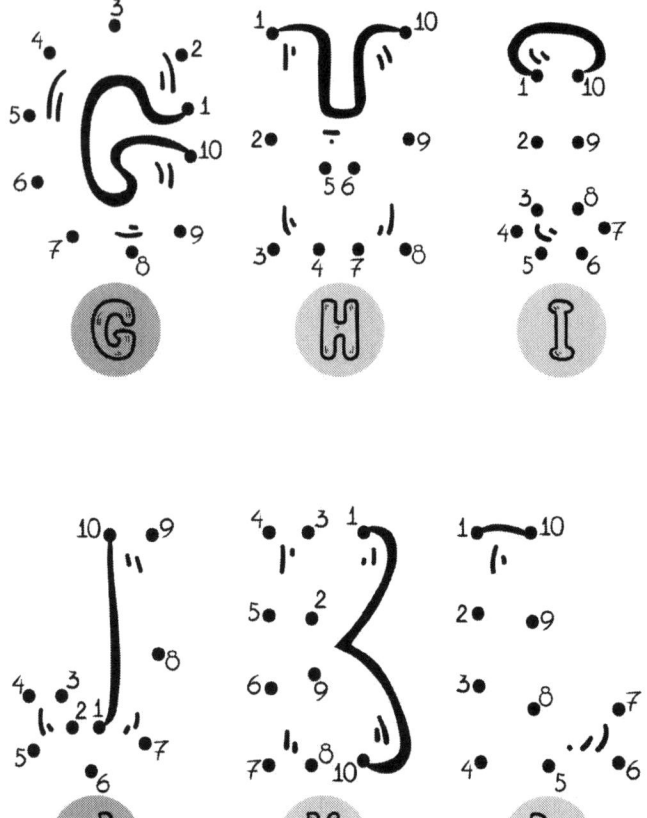

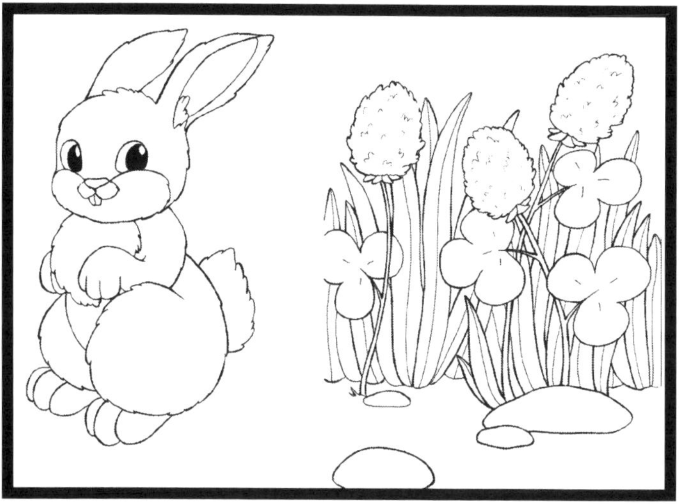

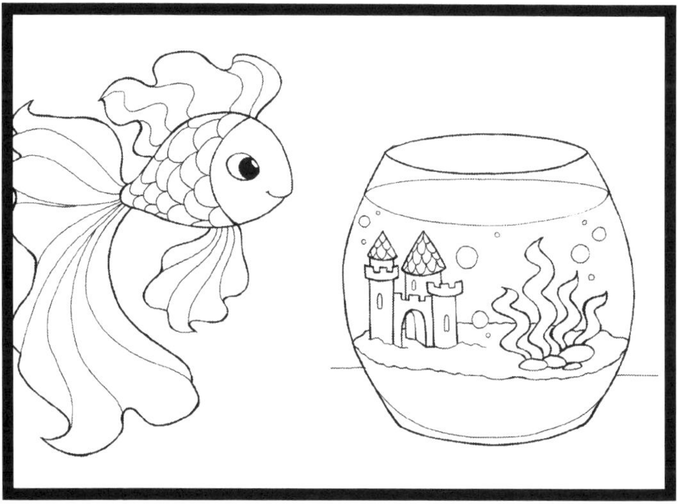

KITTEN

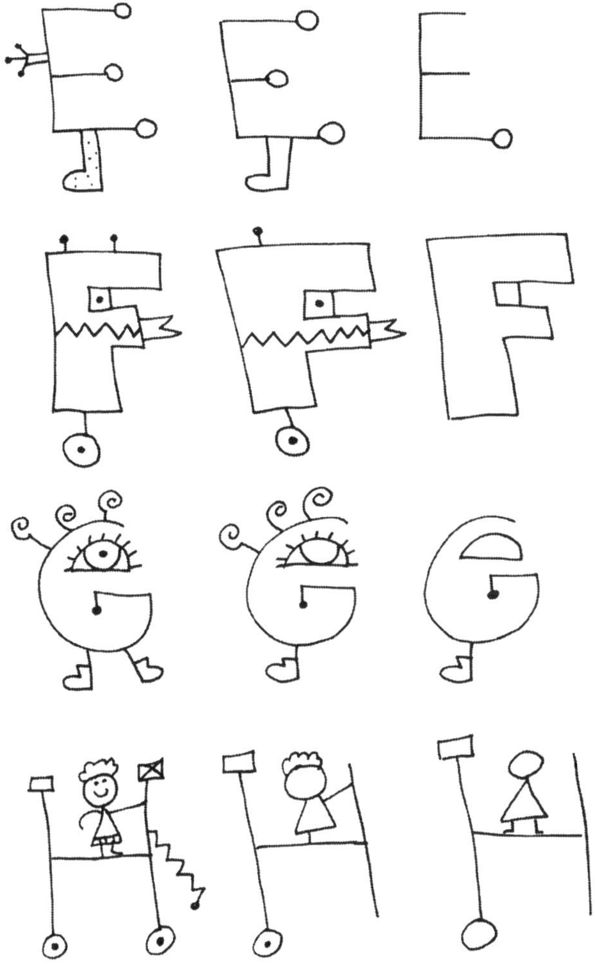

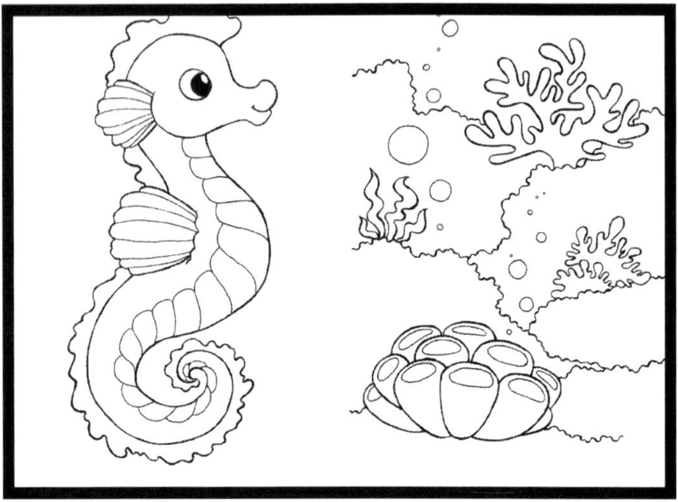

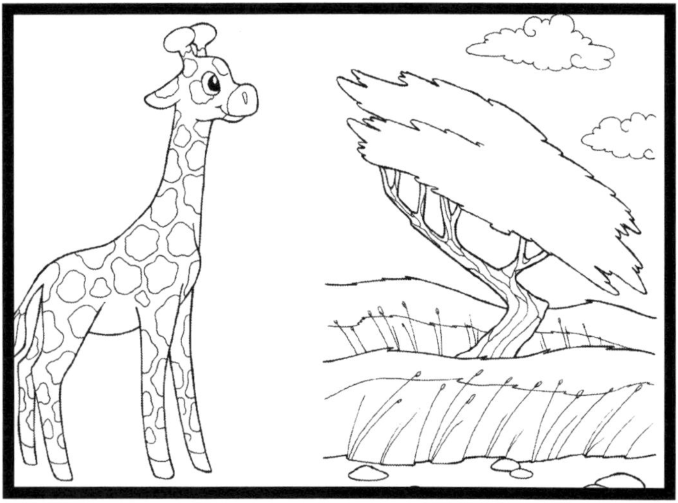

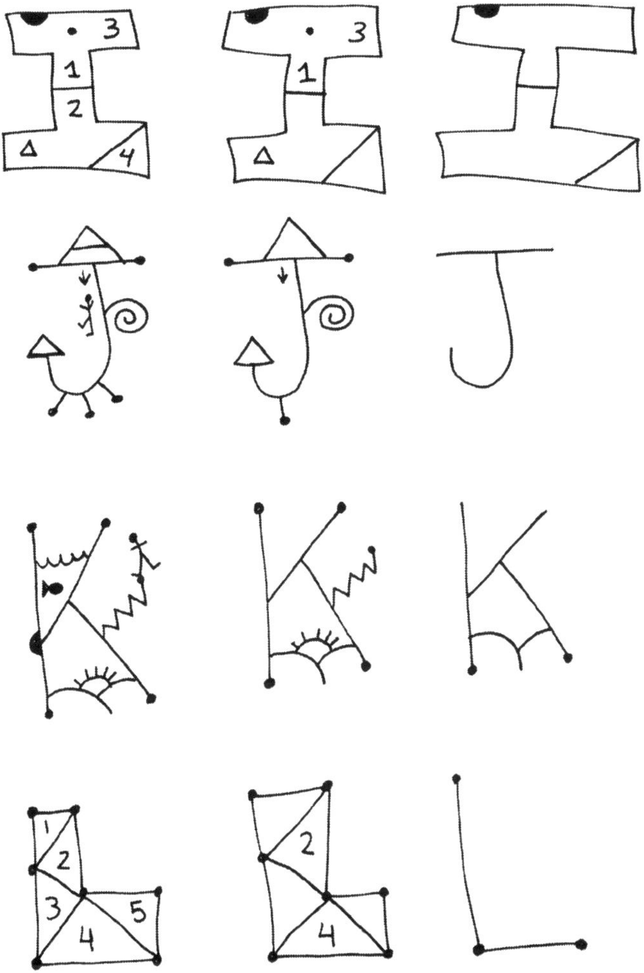

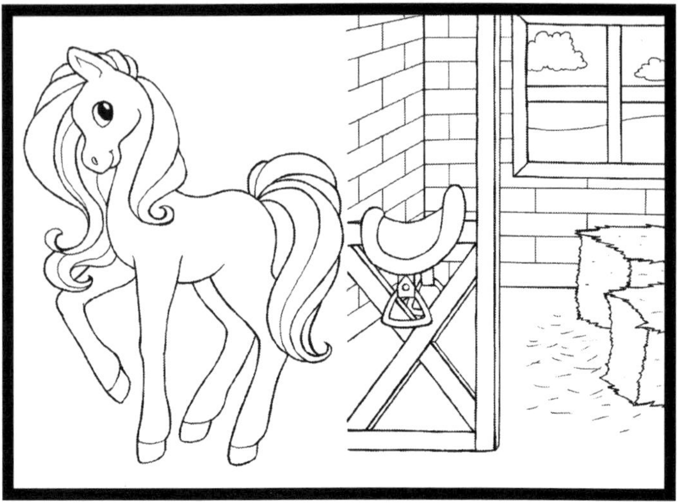

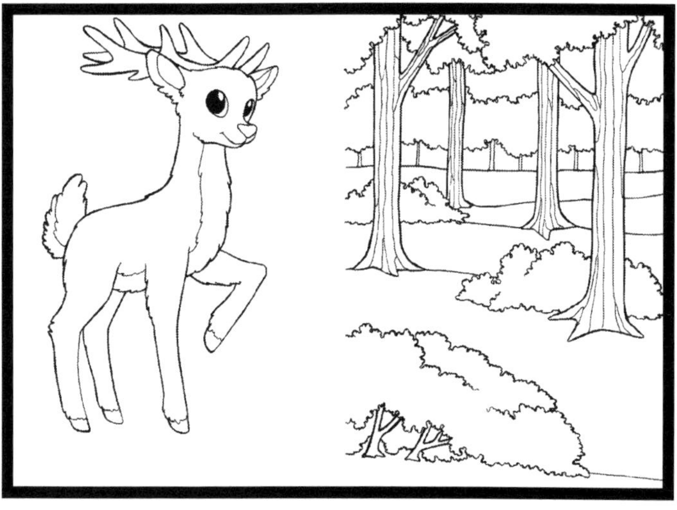

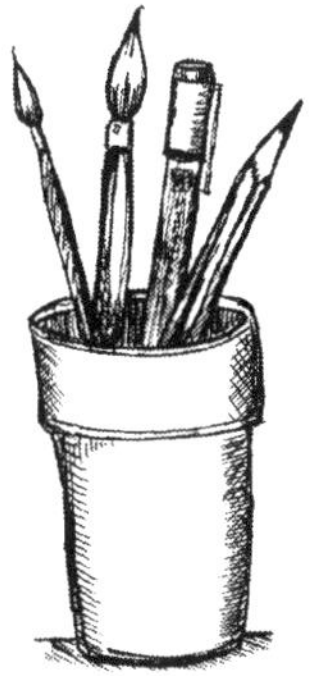

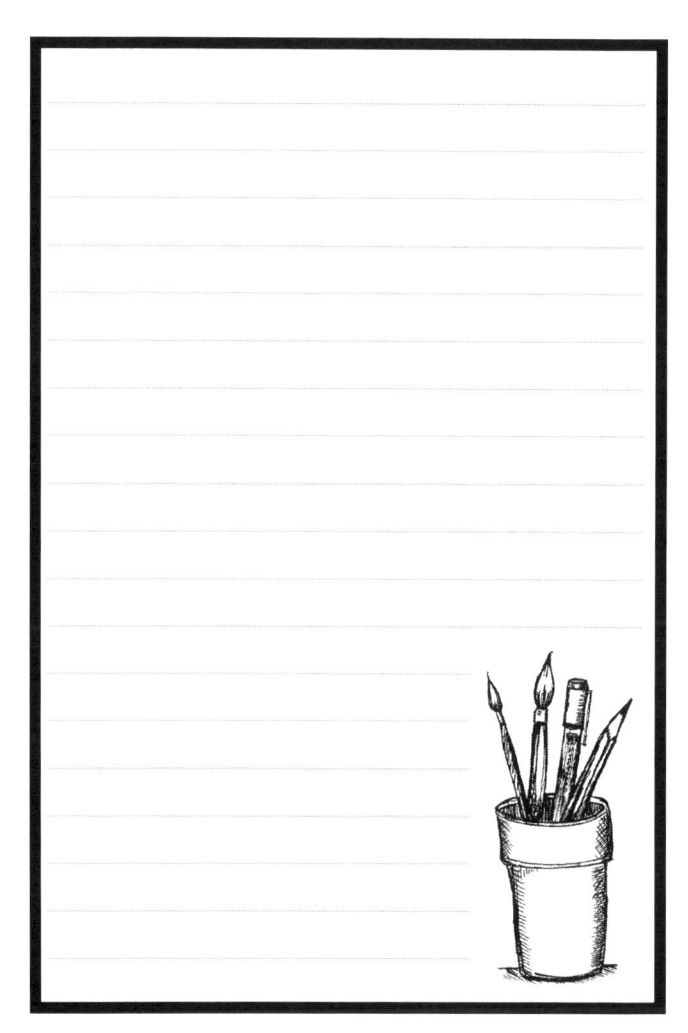

FOX

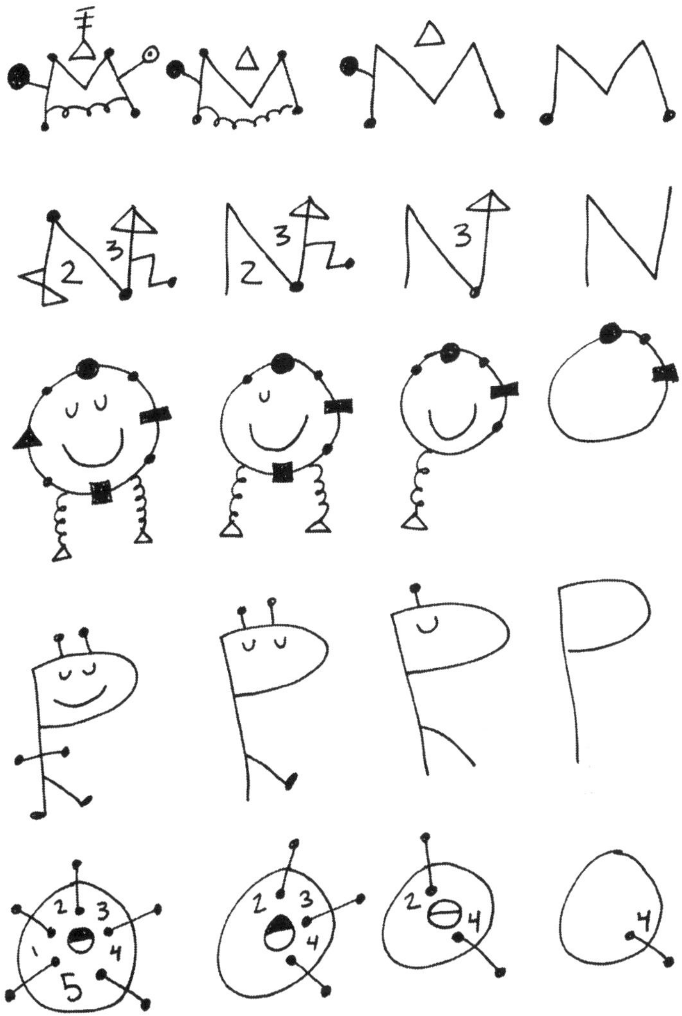

DRAWING TIME

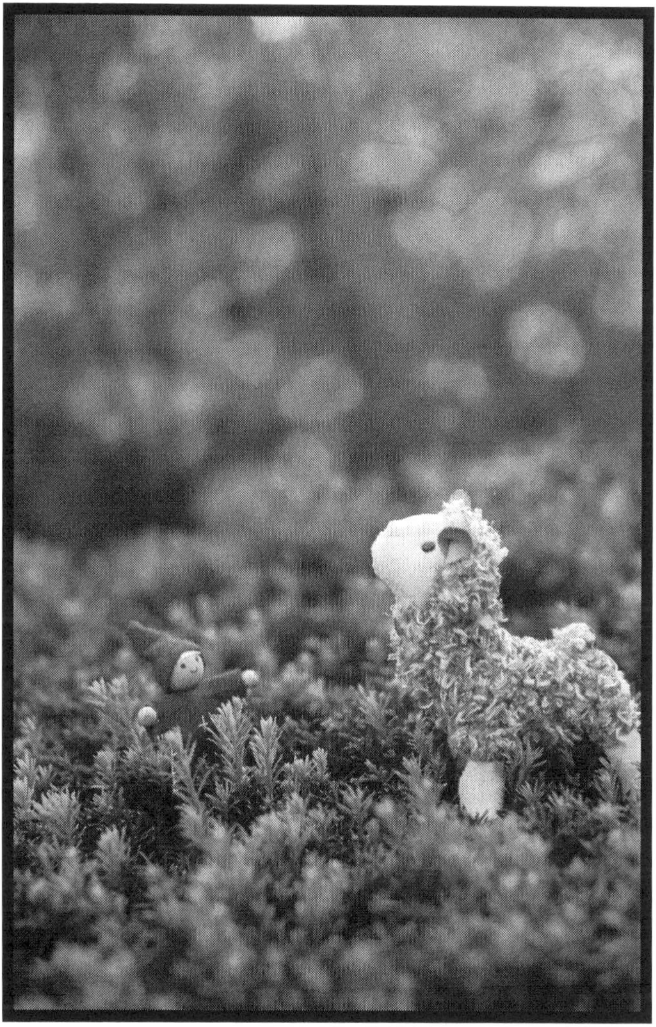

MARY'S LAMB
~SARAH JOSEPHA HALE

Mary had a little lamb,
Its fleece was white as snow,
And everywhere that Mary went
The lamb was sure to go;
He followed her to school one day-
That was against the rule,
It made the children laugh and play
To see a lamb at school.

And so the teacher turned him out,
But still he lingered near,
And waited patiently about,
Till Mary did appear.
And then he ran to her and laid
His head upon her arm,

"What makes the lamb love Mary so?"
The little children cry;
"Oh, Mary loves the lamb, you know,"
The teacher did reply,
"And, you, each gentle animal
In confidence may bind,
And make it follow at your call,
If you are always kind."

LAMB

Sailboat ★

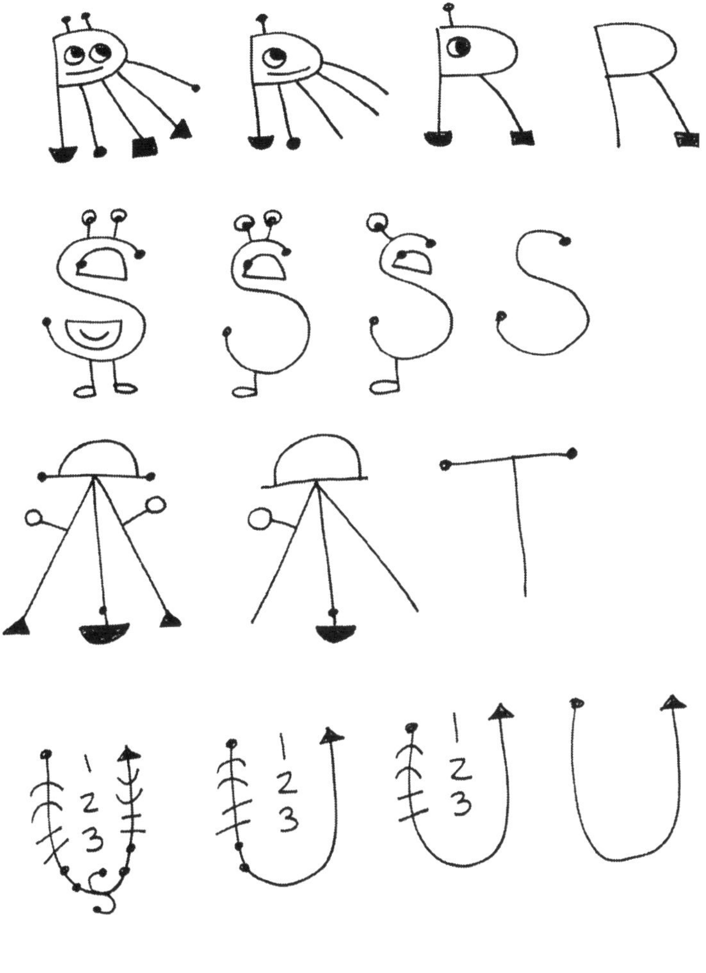
1
2
3
1
2
3
1
2
3

I SPY - FUN-SCHOOLING GAME

Challenge your child to find any item in this picture.

Aa Bb Cc Dd Ee
Ff Gg Hh Ii Jj
Kk Ll Mm Nn
Oo Pp Qq Rr
Ss Tt Uu Vv
Ww Xx Yy Zz

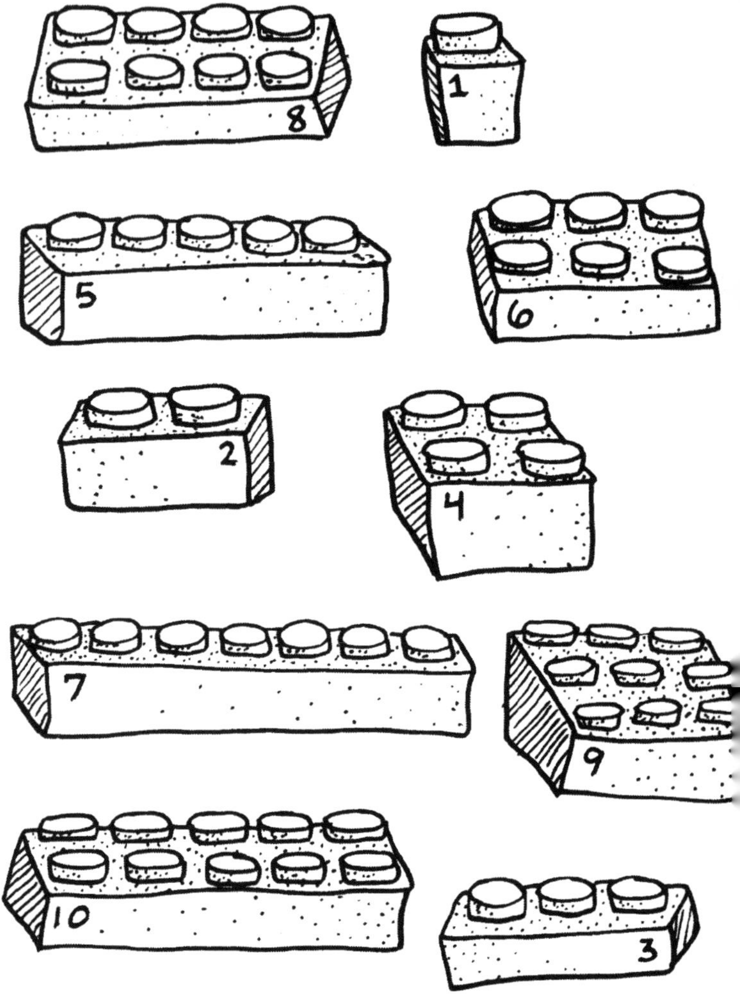
8
1
5
6
2
4
7
9
10
3

0 0 0 0 0 0 0 0 0

1 1 1 1 1 1 1 1 1

2 2 2 2 2 2 2 2 2

3 3 3 3 3 3 3 3 3

4 4 4 4 4 4 4 4 4

5 5 5 5 5 5 5 5 5

6 6 6 6 6 6 6 6 6

7 7 7 7 7 7 7 7 7

8 8 8 8 8 8 8 8 8

9 9 9 9 9 9 9 9 9

DRAWING TIME

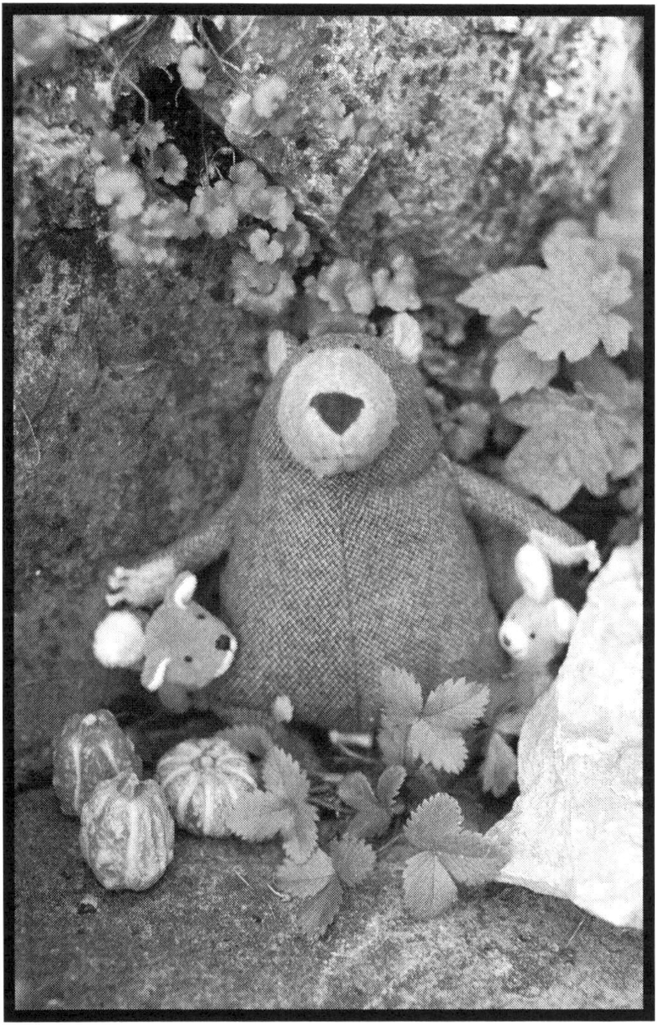

LITTLE

SARAH JANISSE BROWN

Little chipmunk, calm and shy,
I watch you play as I walk by.
Little robin, up so high,
you spread your wings and bravely fly.

Little duckling, swim and play,
with your siblings every day.
Little turtle, so afraid,
in your shell you hide away.

Little puppy, follow me,
come run with me under the trees
Little rabbits wild and free,
cute and fluffy as can be.

Little ants all in a row,
you carry food, oh so slow!
Little bee, where flowers grow,
buzzing, buzzing as you go!

CHIPMUNK

M N O

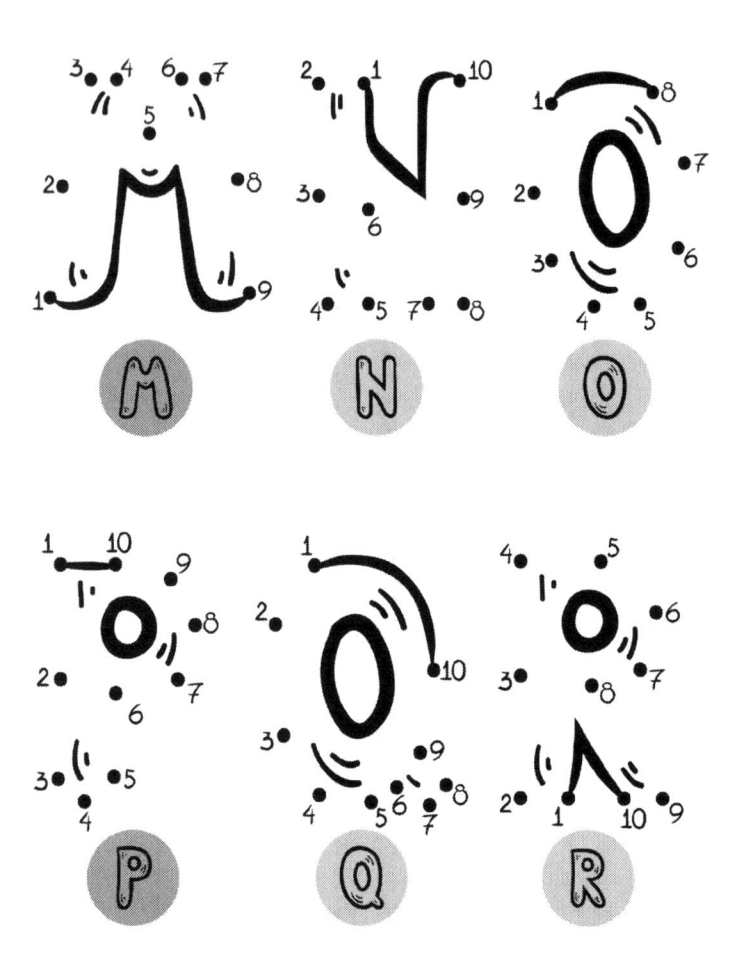

P Q R

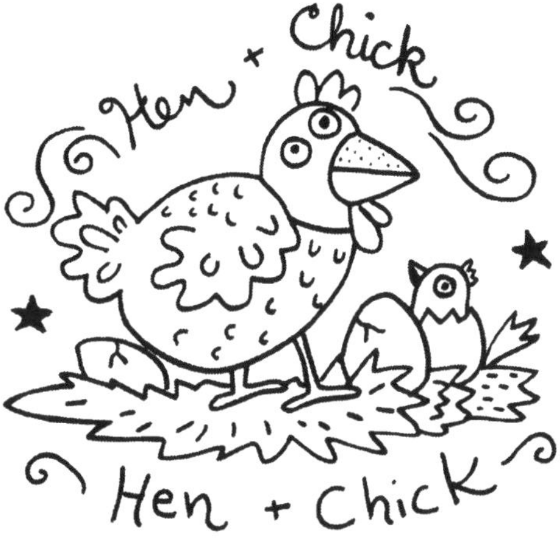
Hen + Chick
Hen + Chick

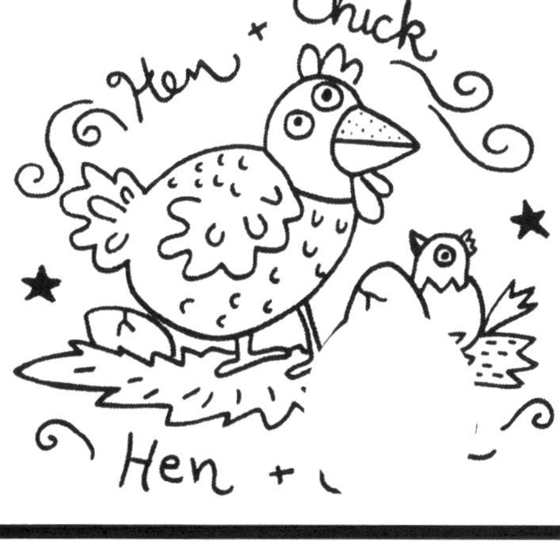
Hen + Chick
Hen +

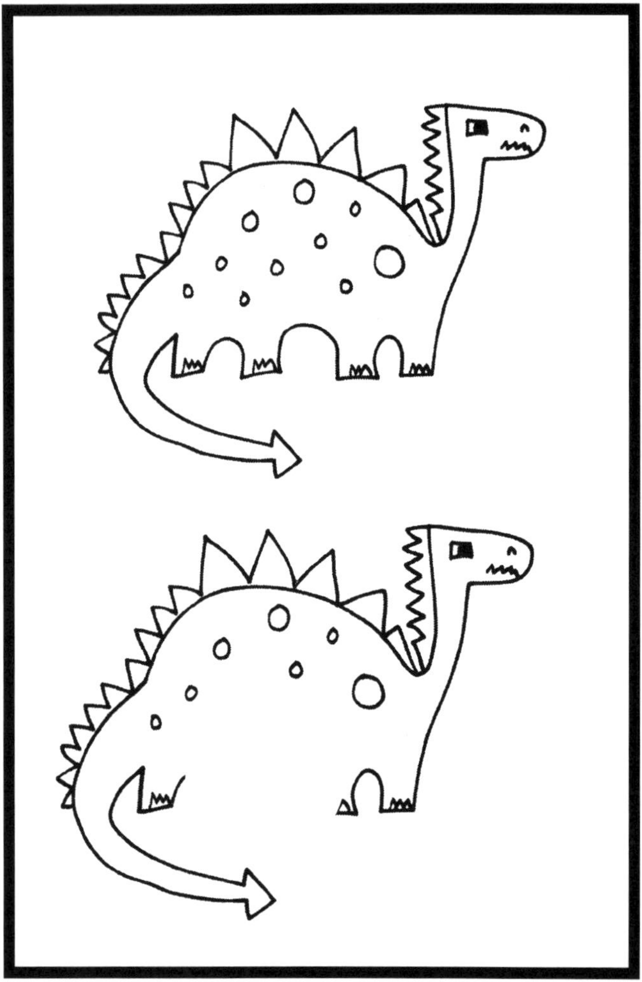

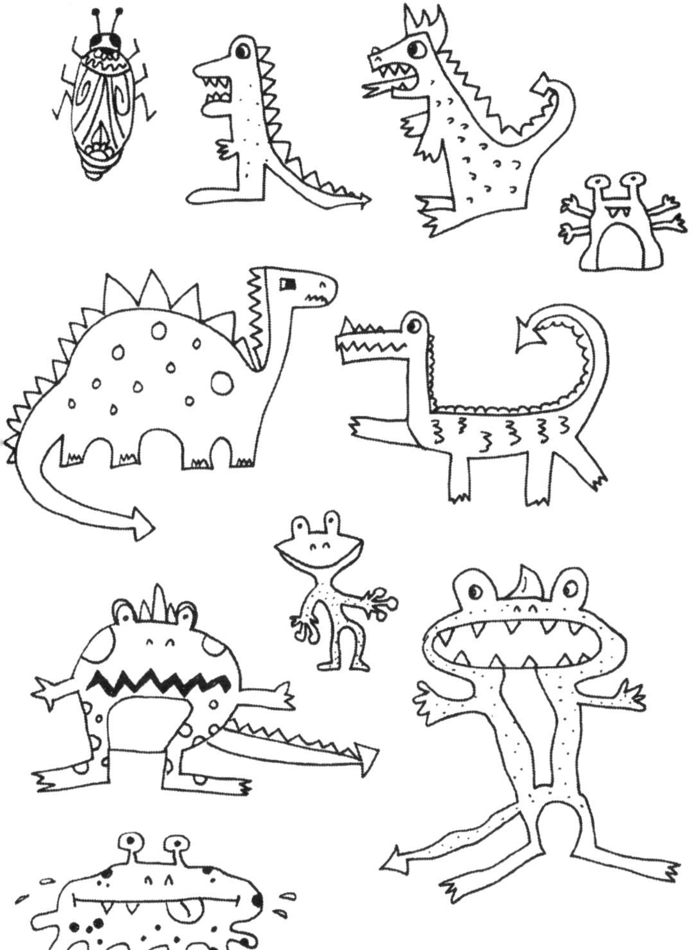

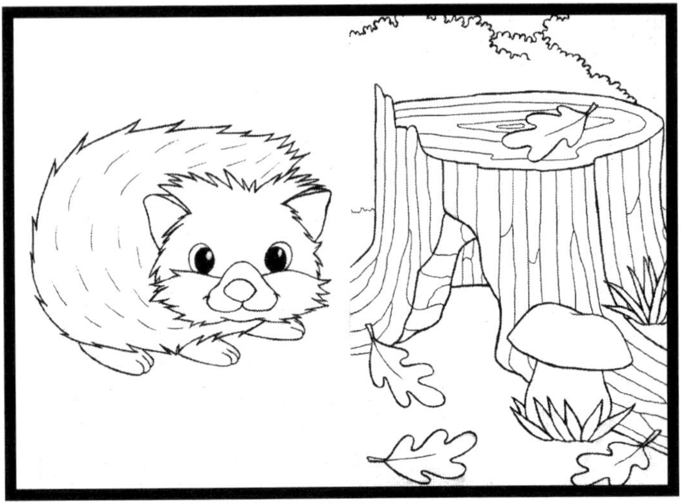

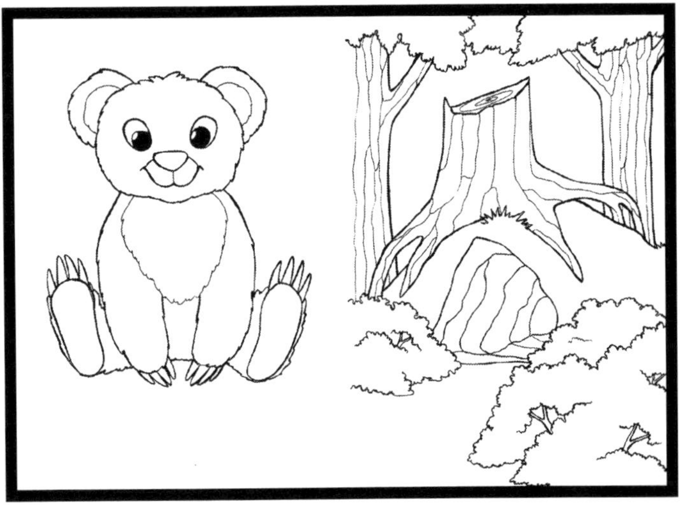

Write down the words of a favorite rhyme.

DRAWING TIME

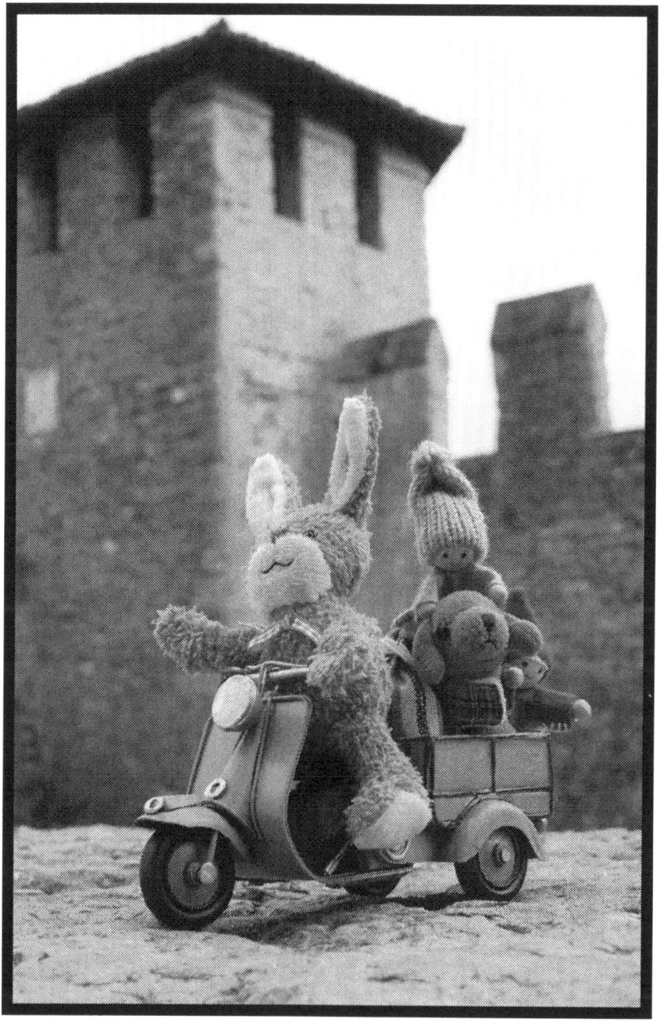

THE COW
~ROBERT LOUIS STEVENSON

The friendly cow, all red and white,
I love with all my heart:
She gives me cream with all her might,
To eat with apple tart.

She wanders lowing here and there,
And yet she cannot stray,
All in the pleasant open air,
The pleasant light of day;

And blown by all the winds that pass
And wet with all the showers,
She walks among the meadow grass
And eats the meadow flowers.

COW

V W X

Aa Bb Cc Dd Ee

Ff Gg Hh Ii Jj

Kk Ll Mm Nn

Oo Pp Qq Rr

Ss Tt Uu Vv

Ww Xx Yy Zz

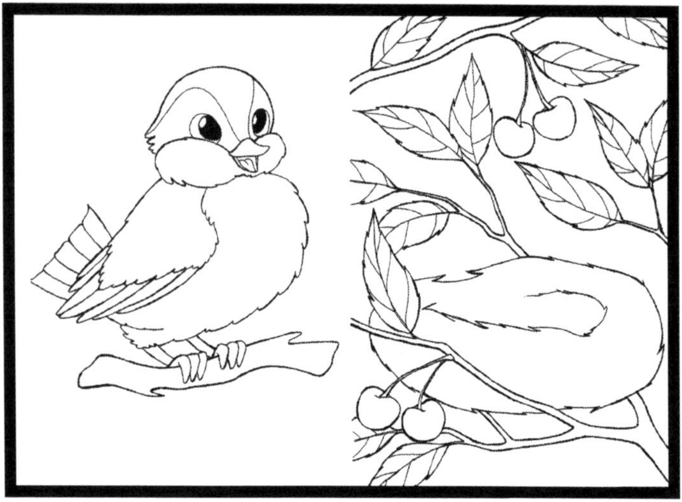

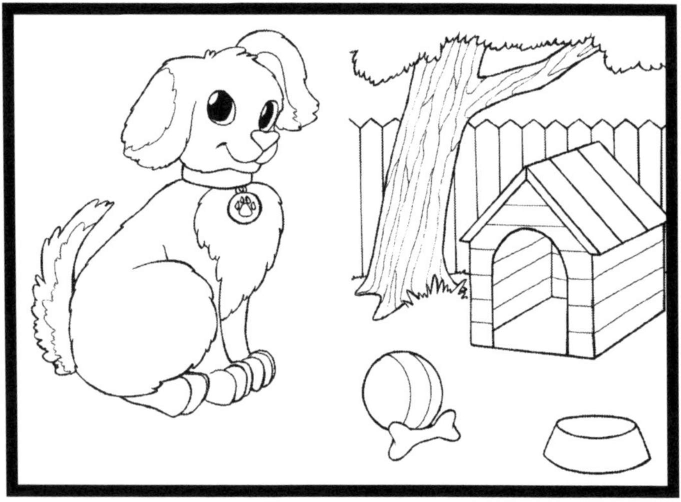

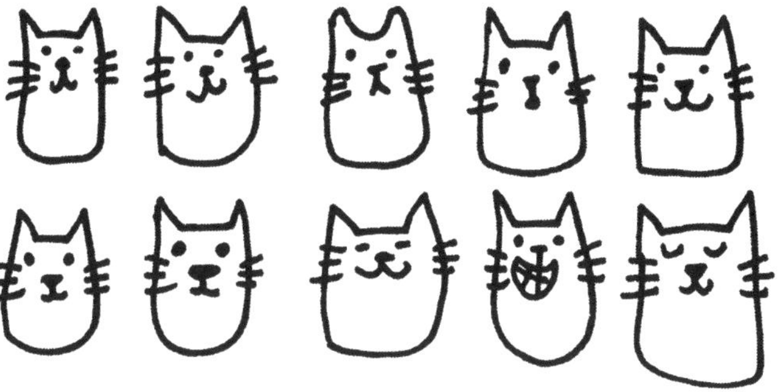

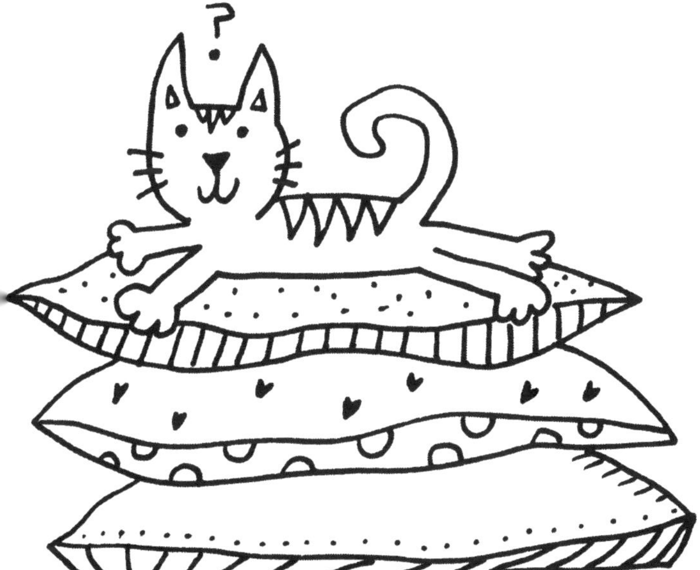

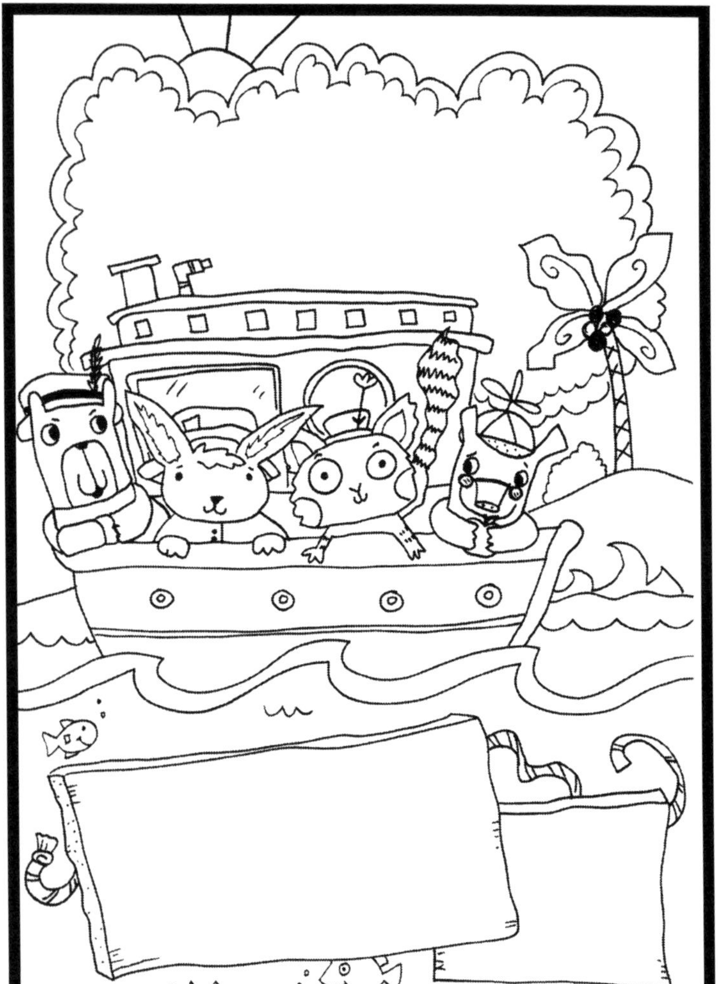

Write a funny letter to your child.

DRAWING TIME

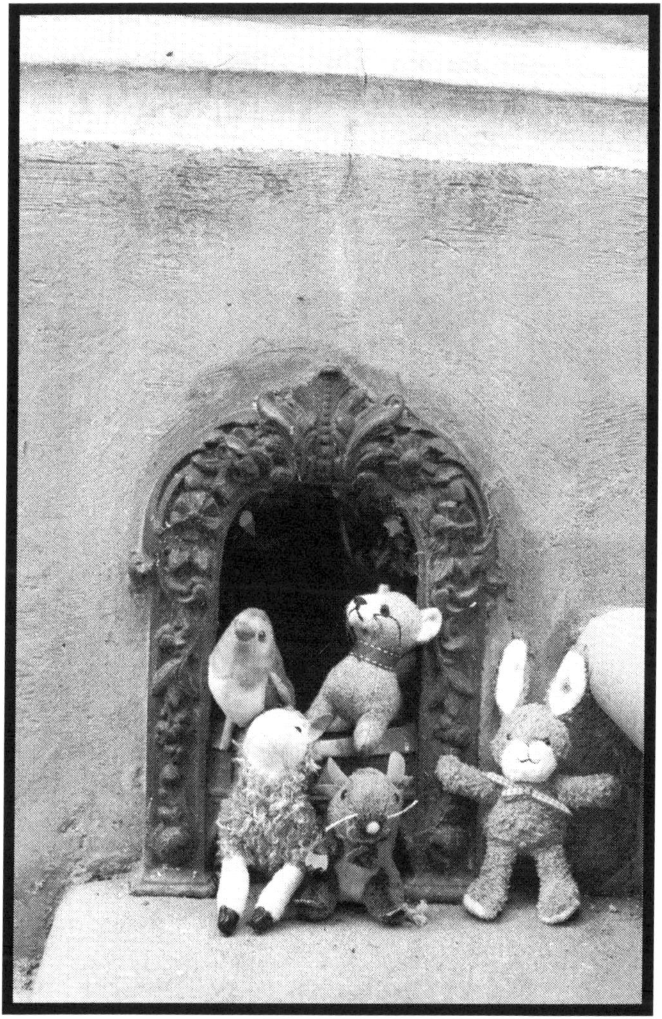

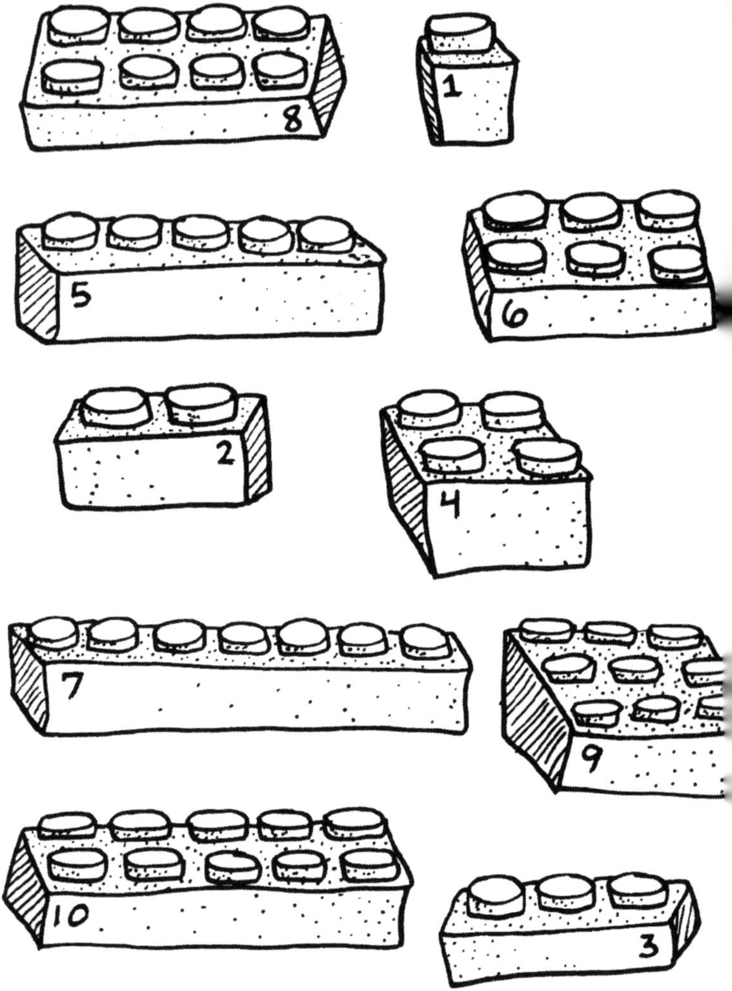
8
1
5
6
2
4
7
9
10
3

0 0 0 0 0 0 0 0 0
1 1 1 1 1 1 1 1 1
2 2 2 2 2 2 2 2 2
3 3 3 3 3 3 3 3 3
4 4 4 4 4 4 4 4 4
5 5 5 5 5 5 5 5 5
6 6 6 6 6 6 6 6 6
7 7 7 7 7 7 7 7 7
8 8 8 8 8 8 8 8 8
9 9 9 9 9 9 9 9 9

Add doodles and colors.

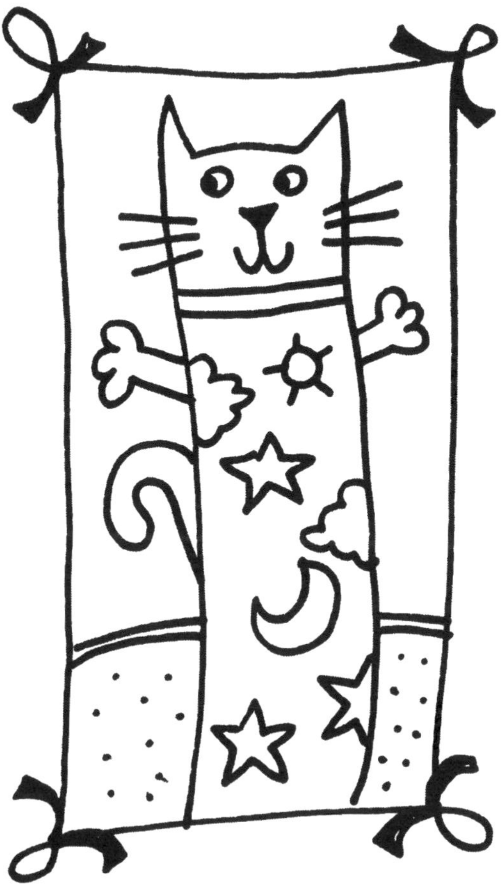

CIRCLE

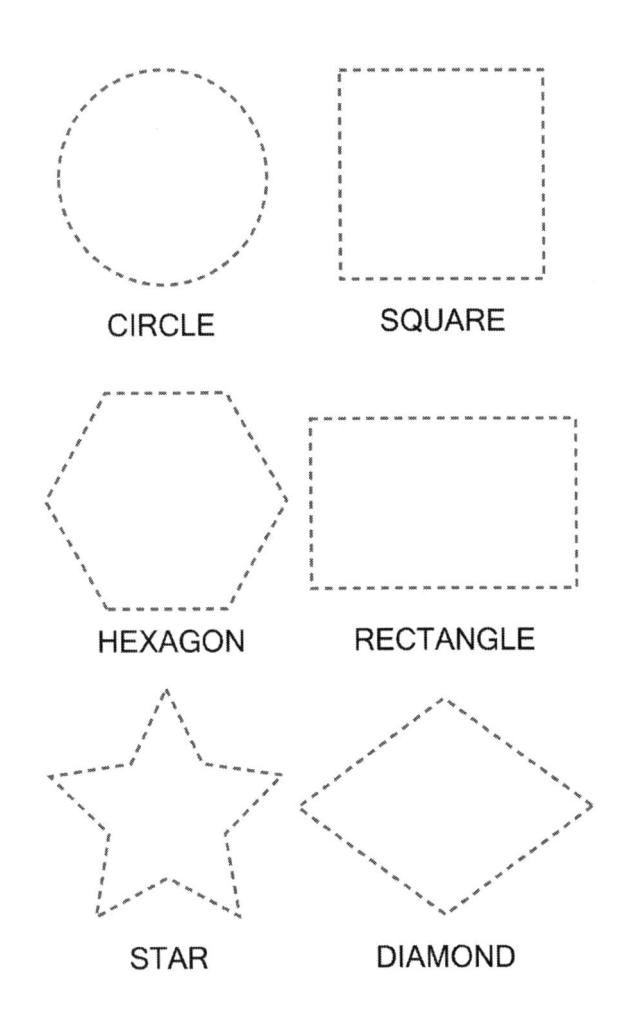

SQUARE

HEXAGON

RECTANGLE

STAR

DIAMOND

ABCDEF
GHIJKL
MNOPQ
RSTUV
WXYZ

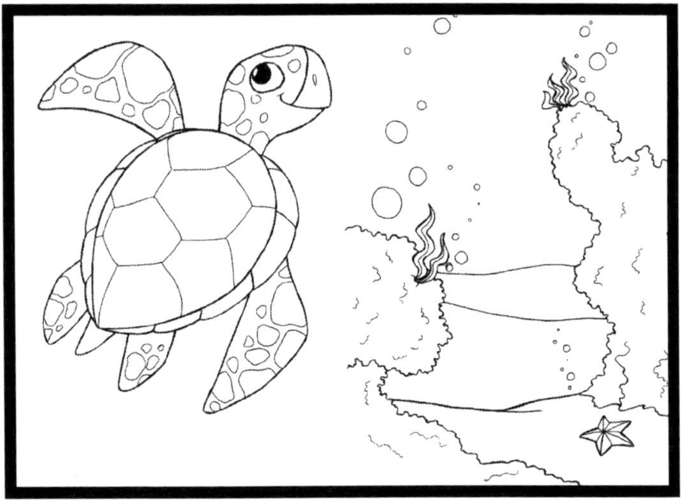

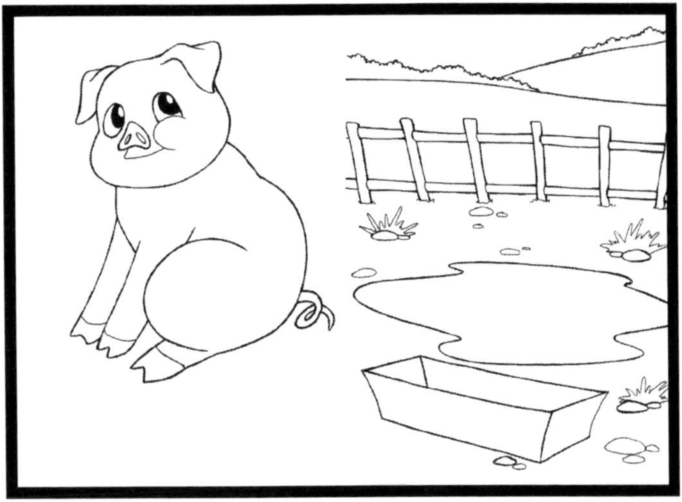

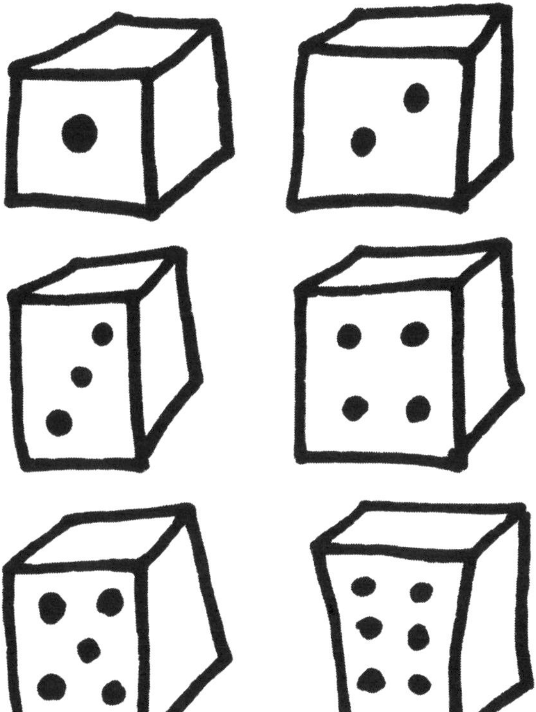

DRAWING TIME

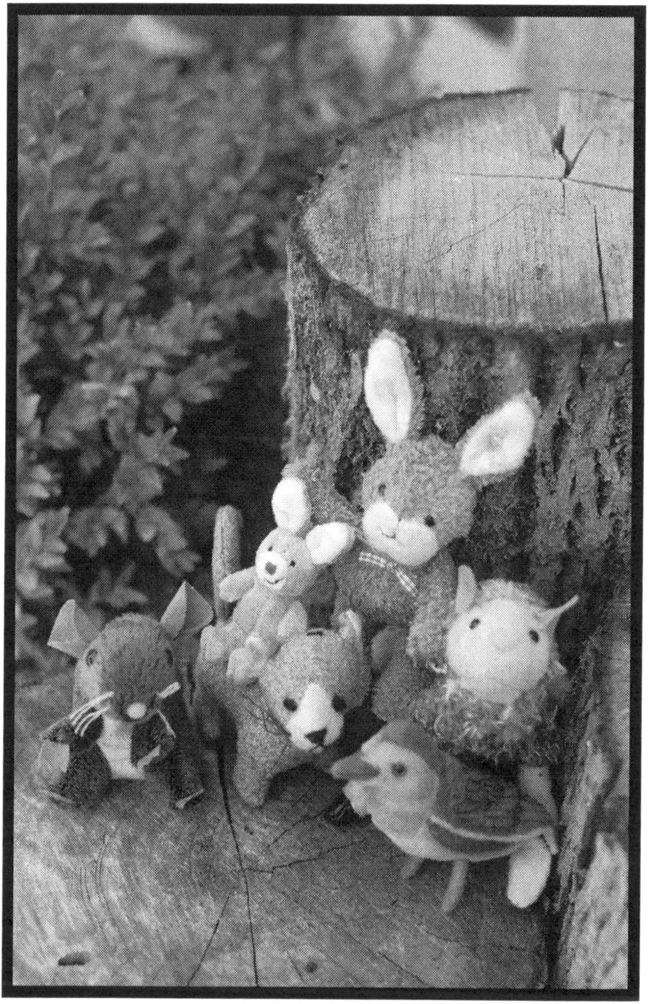

OLD MOTHER HUBBARD AND HER DOG
~SARAH CATHERINE MARINE

Old Mother Hubbard
Went to the cupboard,
To give the poor dog a bone;
When she came there
The cupboard was bare,
And so the poor dog had none.

She went to the baker's
To buy him some bread;
When she came back
The dog was dead.

She went to the undertaker's
To buy him a coffin;
When she came back
The dog was laughing.

She went to the tailor's
To buy him a coat;
When she came back
He was riding a goat.

She went to the cobbler's
To buy him some shoes;
When she came back
He was reading the news.

The dame made a curtsy,
The dog made made a bow;
The dame said, "Your servant,"
The dog said, "Bow-wow."

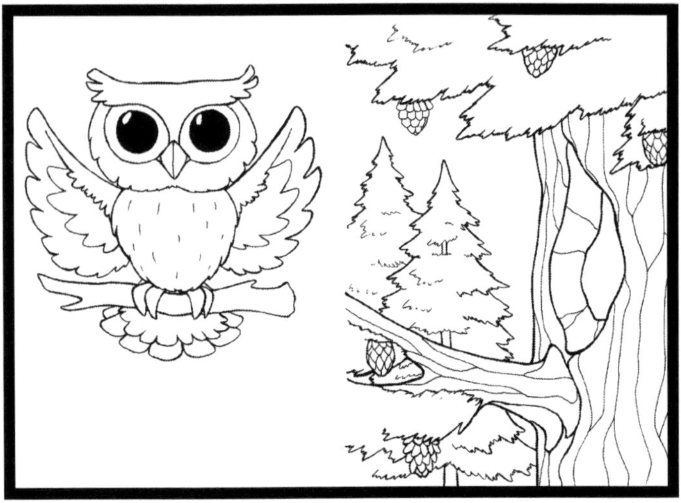

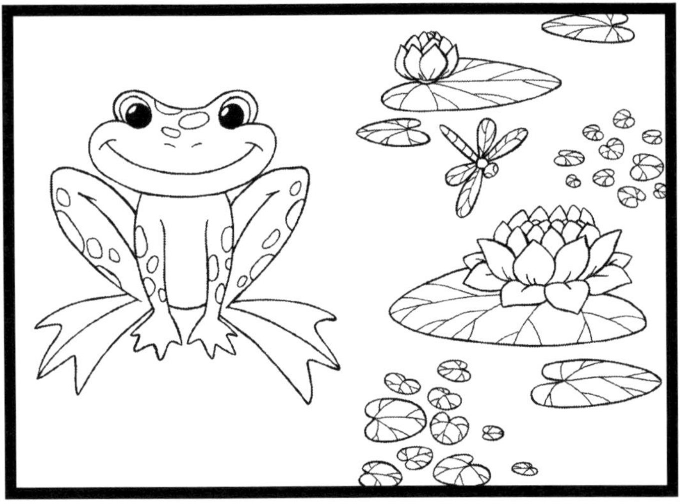

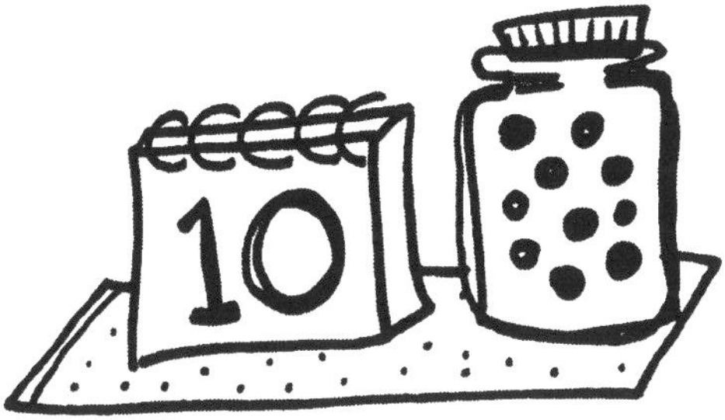
10

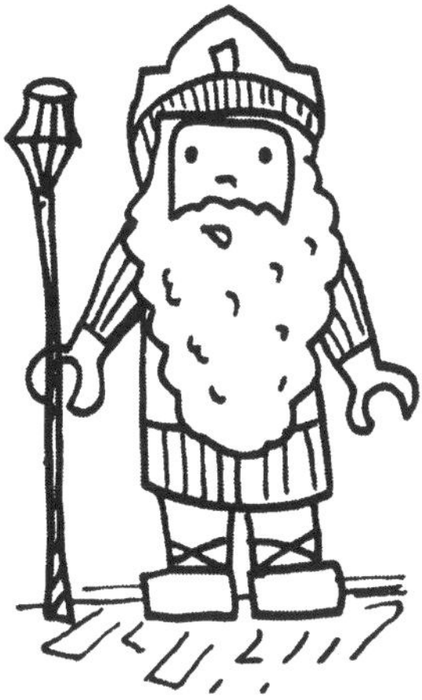

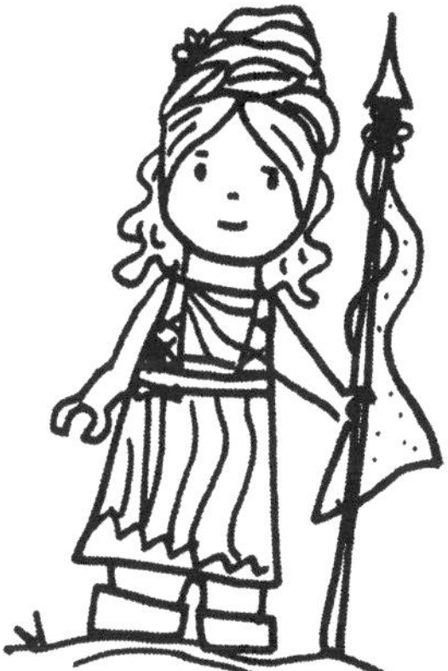

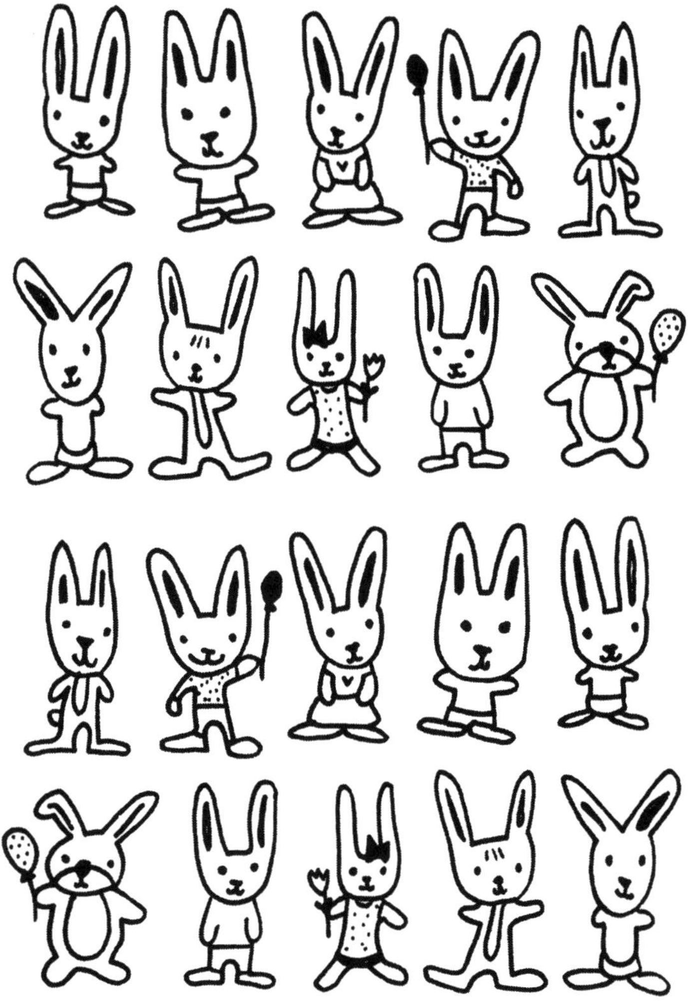

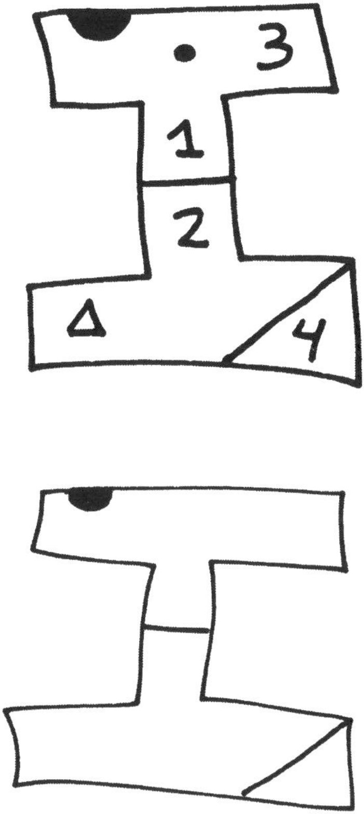
3
1
2
4

AT THE ZOO
~WILLIAM MAKEPEACE THACKERAY

First I saw the white bear, then I saw the black;
Then I saw the camel with a hump upon his back;
Then I saw the grey wolf, with mutton in his maw;
Then I saw the wombat waddle in the straw;
Then I saw the elephant a-waving of his trunk;
Then I saw the monkeys-mercy, how unpleasantly they-smelt!

BEAR

DRAWING TIME

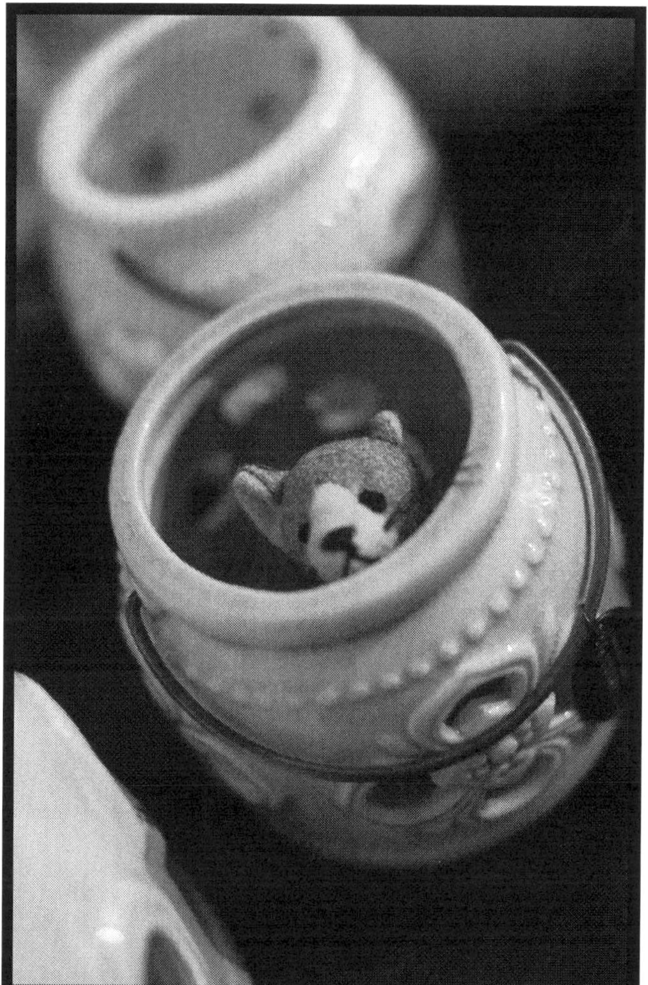

Aa Bb Cc Dd Ee

Ff Gg Hh Ii Jj

Kk Ll Mm Nn

Oo Pp Qq Rr

Ss Tt Uu Vv

Ww Xx Yy Zz

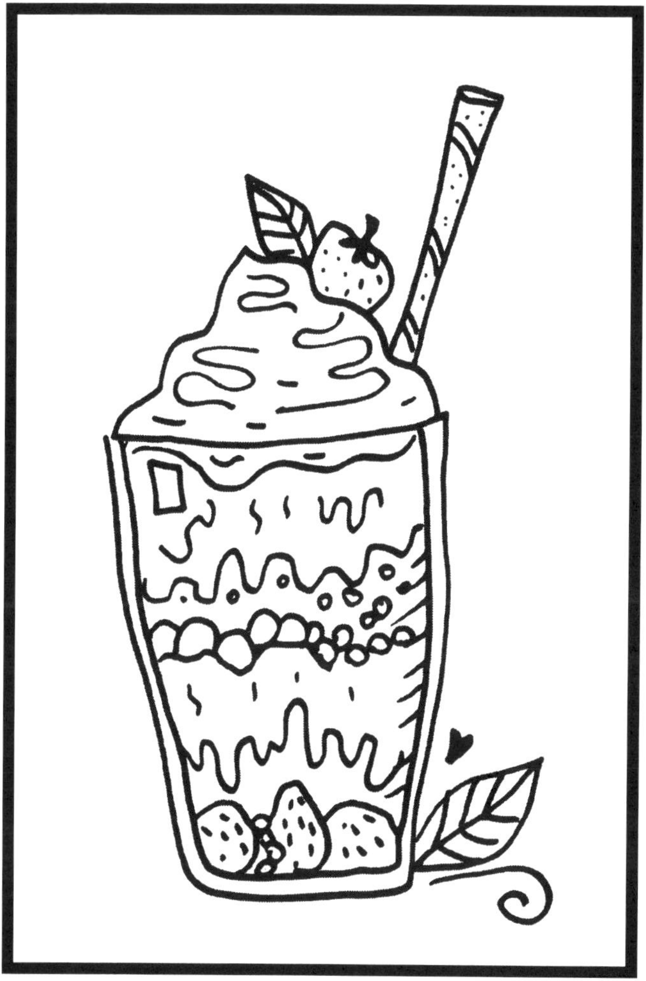

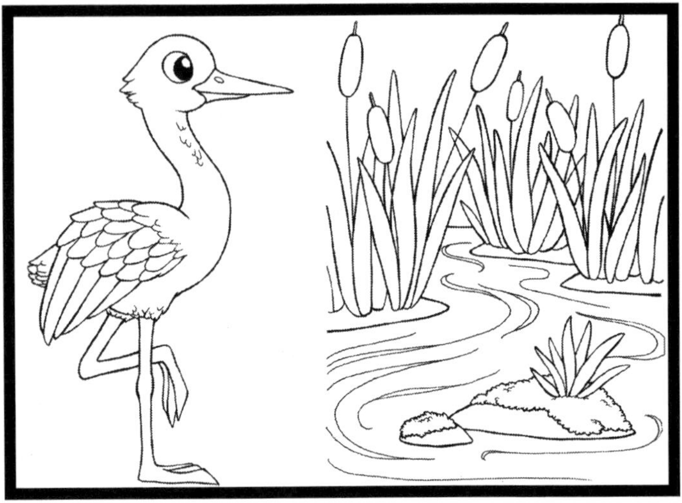

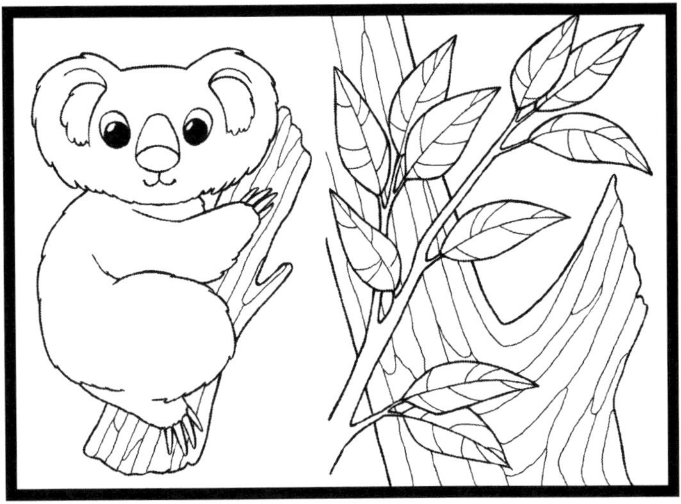

FRIENDLY DUCKLING
SARAH JANISSE BROWN

Friendly ducking follow me
to the pond, and to the creek.
Friendly duckling we will play
splashing, quacking every day.

Fluffy, yellow, soft and cute
I just want to play with you.
Little duckling follow me
to the pond, and to the creek.

We'll have a picnic at two,
and I'll share my lunch with you.
I'll bring grapes and little seeds,
If you would like to share with me.

DUCK

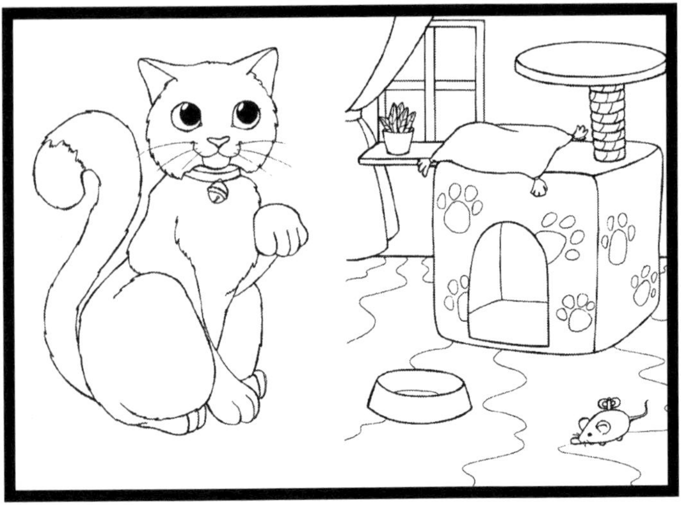

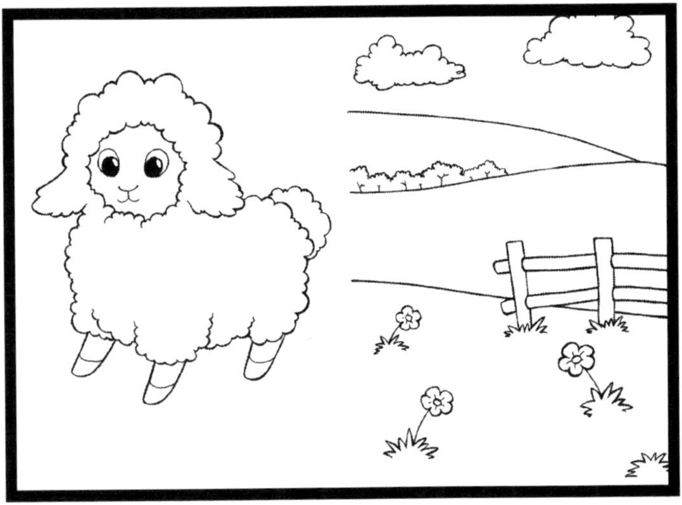

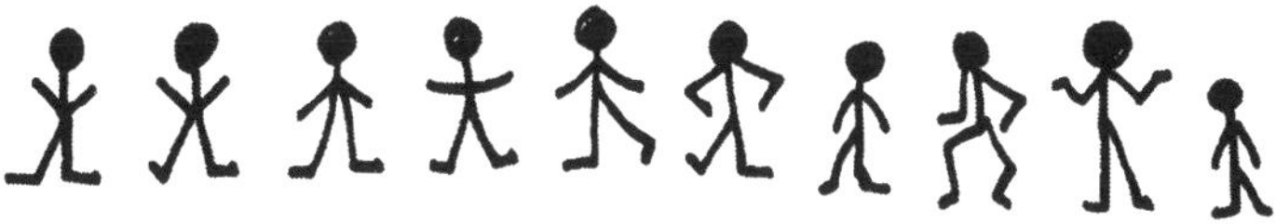

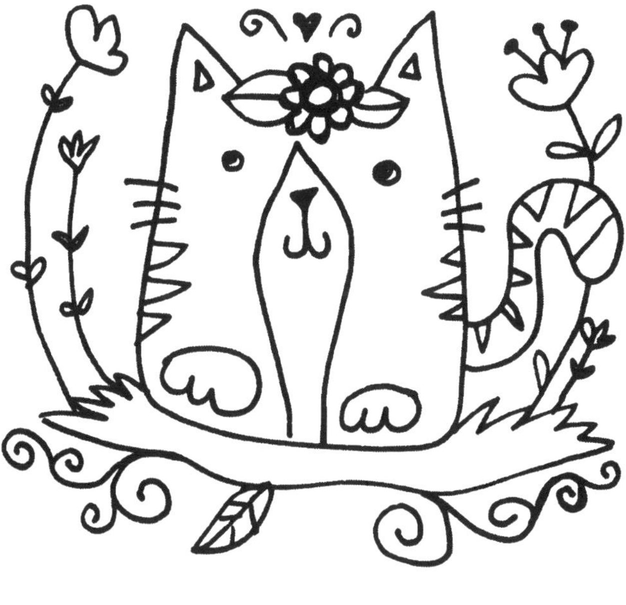

DRAWING TIME

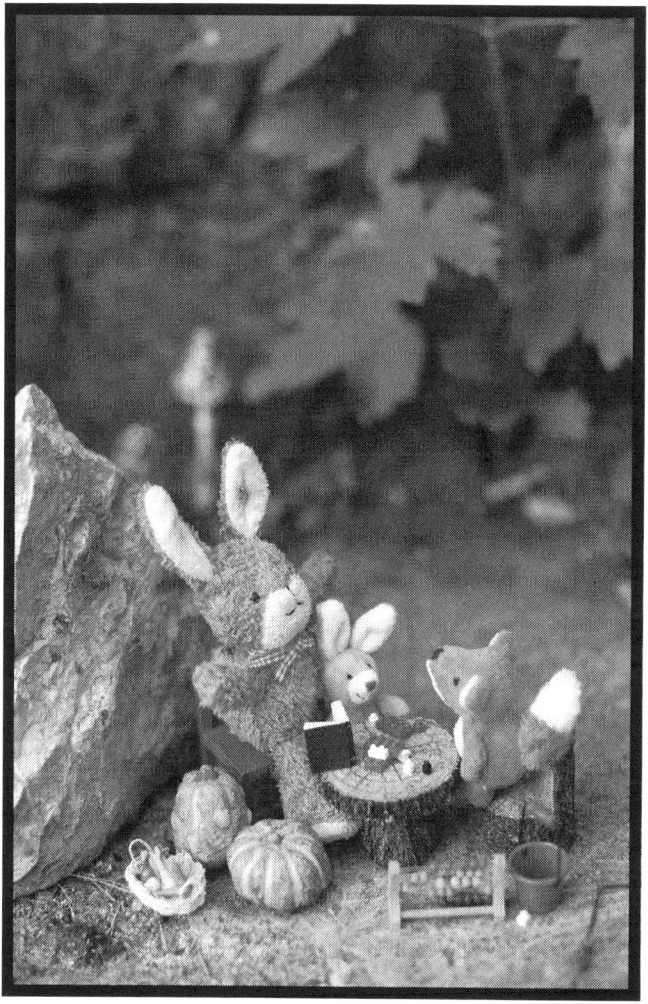

GOAT

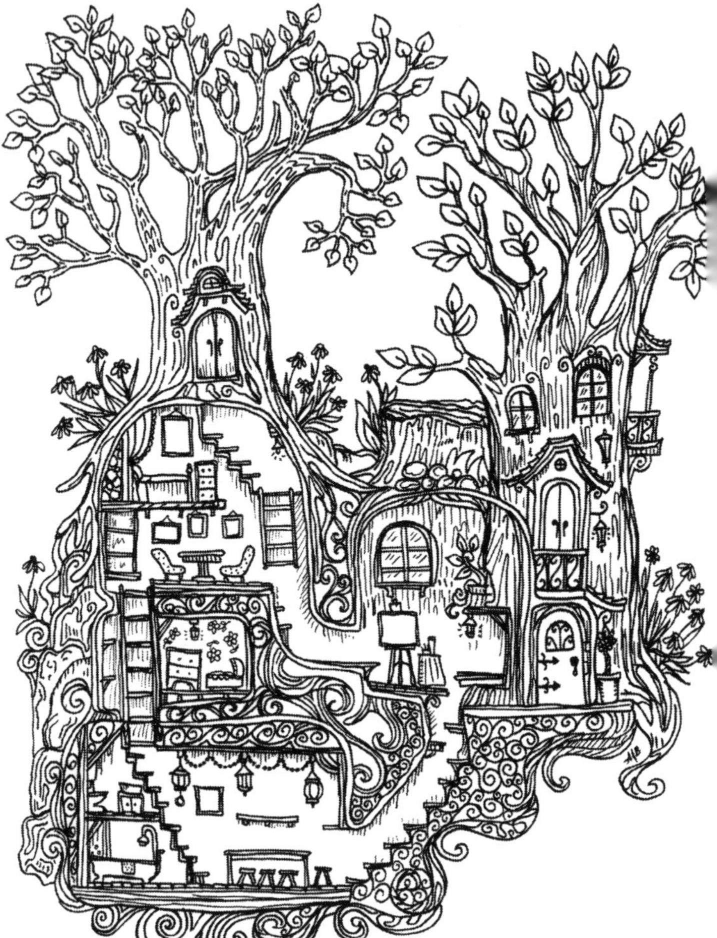

TREES

~SARAH COLERIDGE

The Oak is called the king of trees,
The Aspen quivers in the breeze,
The Poplar grows up straight and tall,
The Peach tree spreads along the wall,
The Sycamore gives pleasant shade,
The Willow droops in watery glade,
The Fir tree useful in timber gives,
The Beech amid the forest lives.

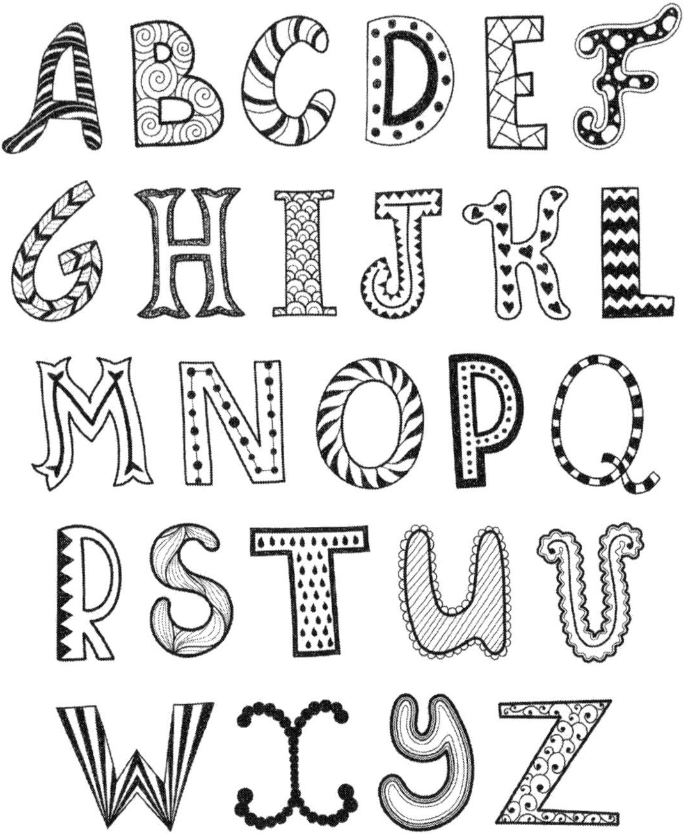
ABCDEF
GHIJKL
MNOPQ
RSTUV
WXYZ

DRAWING TIME

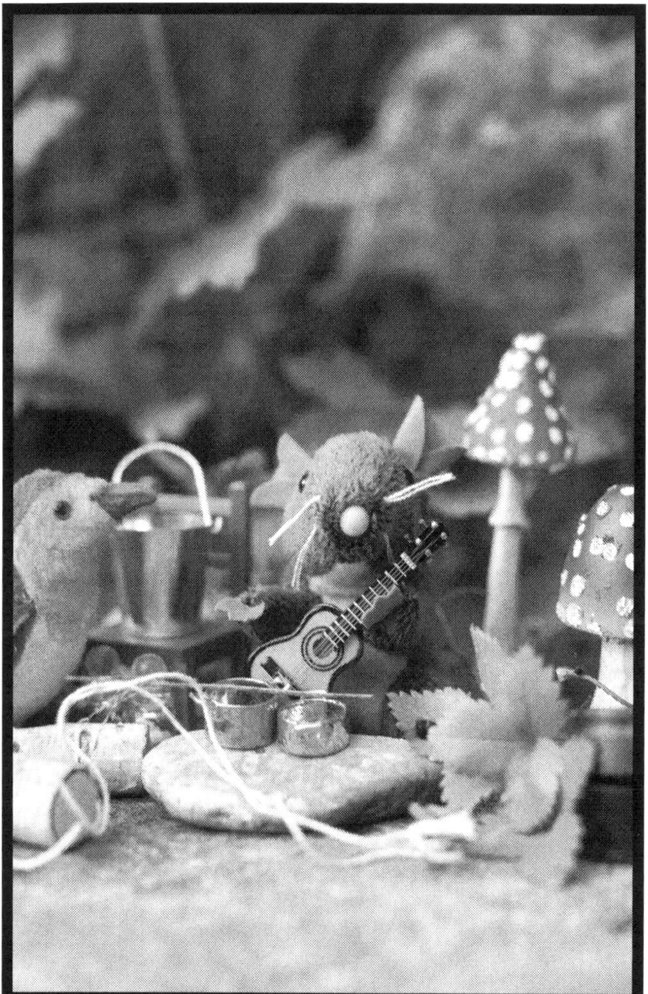

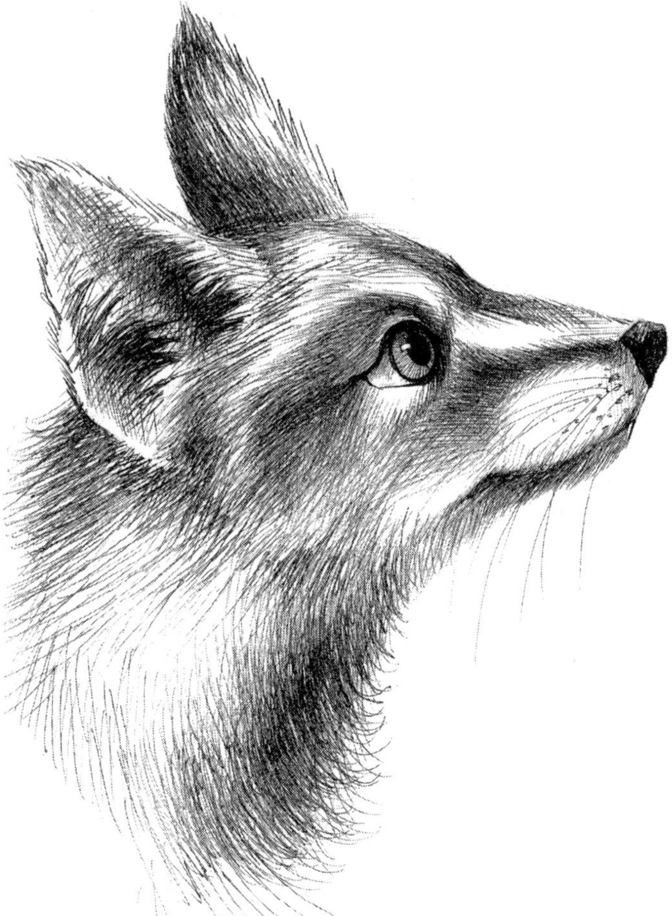

I SPY - FUN-SCHOOLING GAME

CHALLeNGe your child to FiNd aNy iteM iN this picture.

Published by: The Thinking Tree, LLC
Artwork by Tolik Trishkin, Tanya Hulinska, Anastasia Fitas
& Sarah Janisse Brown
Copyright 2017—Do Not Copy
FunSchoolingBooks.com

Made in the USA
Middletown, DE
13 February 2019